OCEAN ANIMALS FOR KIDS

OCEAN ANIMALS FOR KIDS

A JUNIOR SCIENTIST'S GUIDE
to Whales, Sharks, and Other Marine Life

BETHANIE AND JOSH HESTERMANN

ROCKRIDGE PRESS

To Forest, our newest little adventurer

For general information on our other products and services or to obtain technical support, please contact our Customer Care Department within the United States at (866) 744-2665, or outside the United States at (510) 253-0500.

Rockridge Press publishes its books in a variety of electronic and print formats. Some content that appears in print may not be available in electronic books, and vice versa.

Series Designer: Junior Scientist Design Team
Interior and Cover Designer: Emma Hall
Art Producer: Tom Hood
Editor: Mary Colgan
Production Manager: Riley Hoffman
Production Editor: Sigi Nacson

Illustrations @ Kate Francis, 2020. Photography John Shaw/Science Source, pp. ii, 17, 19; robertharding/Alamy, pp. vi, 13; Shane Partridge/Alamy, p. 2; National Geographic Image Collection/Alamy, pp. 6, 7; Juergen Schonnop/Alamy, p. 8; Imagebroker/Alamy, pp. 9, 14, 30, 31, 40, 56, 47, 53; BIOSPHOTO/Alamy, p. 11; Martin Strmiska/Alamy, p. 12; Kevin Schafer/Alamy, p. 15; B & C Alexander/Science Source, p. 16; Dotted Zebra/Alamy, p. 18; Art Wolfe/Science Source, p. 20; SuperStock/Alamy, p. 21; Reinhard Dirscherl/Alamy, pp. 22, 23; Seaphotoart/Alamy, p. 24; SPL/Science Source, pp. 25, 51; Michael Patrick O'Neill/Alamy, pp. 27, 41, 55; Andrey Nekrasov/Alamy, p. 28; Nature Picture Library/Alamy, pp. 29, 42; David Fleetham/Alamy, pp. 32, 43; WaterFrame/Alamy, p. 33; Blue Planet Archive/Alamy, pp. 34, 35; mauritius images GmbH/Alamy, p. 38; MichaelGrantWildlife/Alamy, p. 39; Charles Stirling (Diving)/Alamy, pp. 44, 45; Julie Huser/Alamy, p. 46; Joseph S Giacalone, p. 48; Science Source, p. 50; John Anderson/Alamy, p. 52; Juergen Freund/alamy, p. 54; cbimages/Alamy, p. 57; Niebrugge Images/Alamy, p. 58; AF Archive/Alamy, p. 59; Francois Gohier/Science Source, p. 60. Author photograph courtesy Genevieve Elaine Photography.

Page ii: Adélie penguins, page 20

ISBN: Print 978-1-64876-056-3
eBook 978-1-64876-057-0
R0

Printed in China

CONTENTS

Garibaldi fish and starfish in a kelp forest

WELCOME, JUNIOR SCIENTIST!

Ocean life is as marvelous as it is mysterious. It's as wonderful as it is weird. Whether you like eels or seals, whales or snails, you've come to the right place. In this Junior Scientist's Guide, you'll learn about the ocean and the animals that live in and around it. You'll learn answers to questions you didn't even know you had, like "How do sponges breathe?" and "Which **marine** animal has pink poop?" Throughout the book, you'll see words in **bold** like the word *marine* on this page. This means you can find a definition in the glossary on page 63.

As you explore, remember how important you are in protecting the ocean and all marine life. Even taking small steps to use less plastic or less electricity can make a big difference for the planet we all share. And now, it's time to dive in. Welcome, Junior Scientist! There is so much to discover!

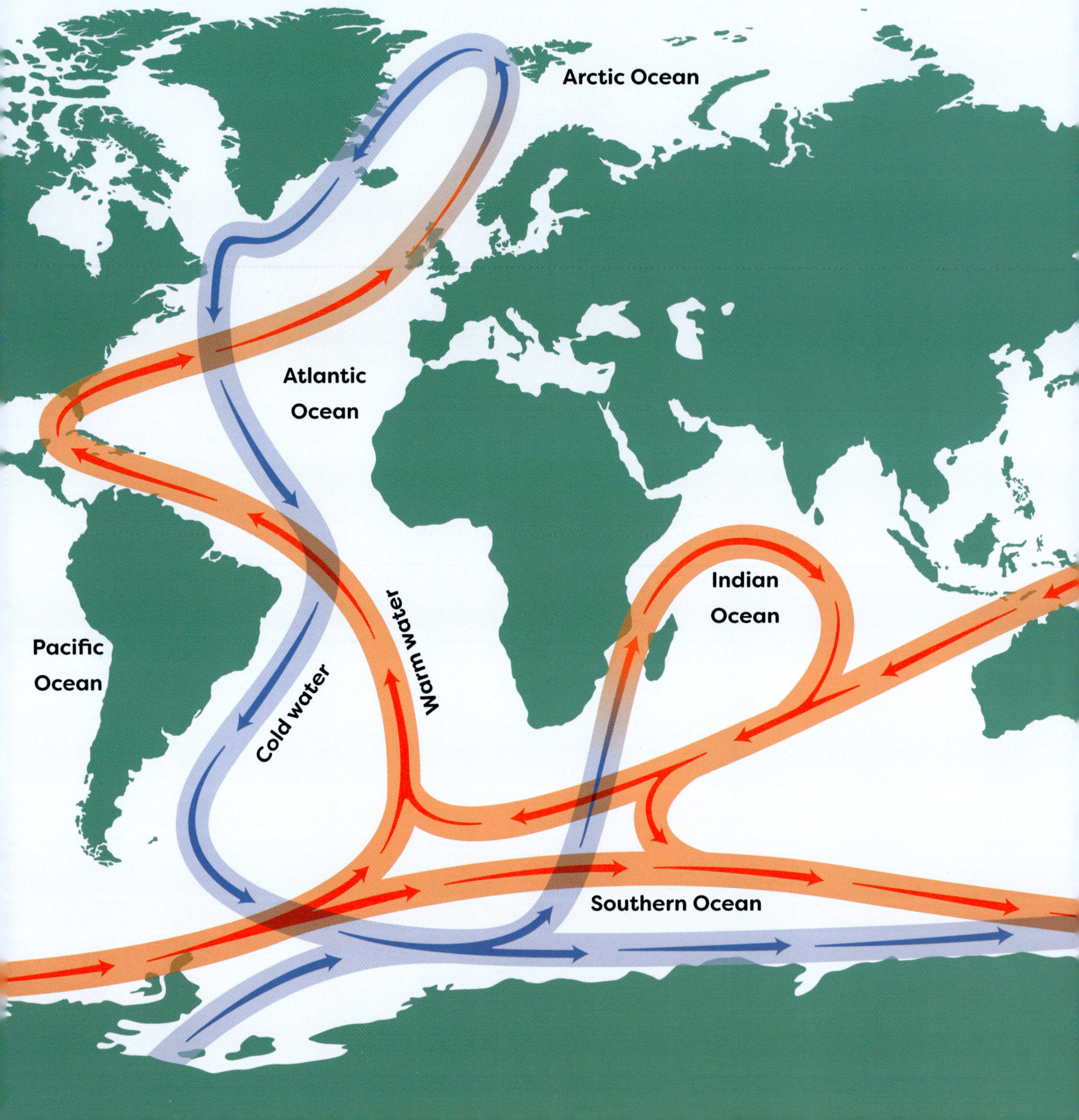

Arctic Ocean
Atlantic Ocean
Pacific Ocean
Indian Ocean
Southern Ocean
Cold water
Warm water

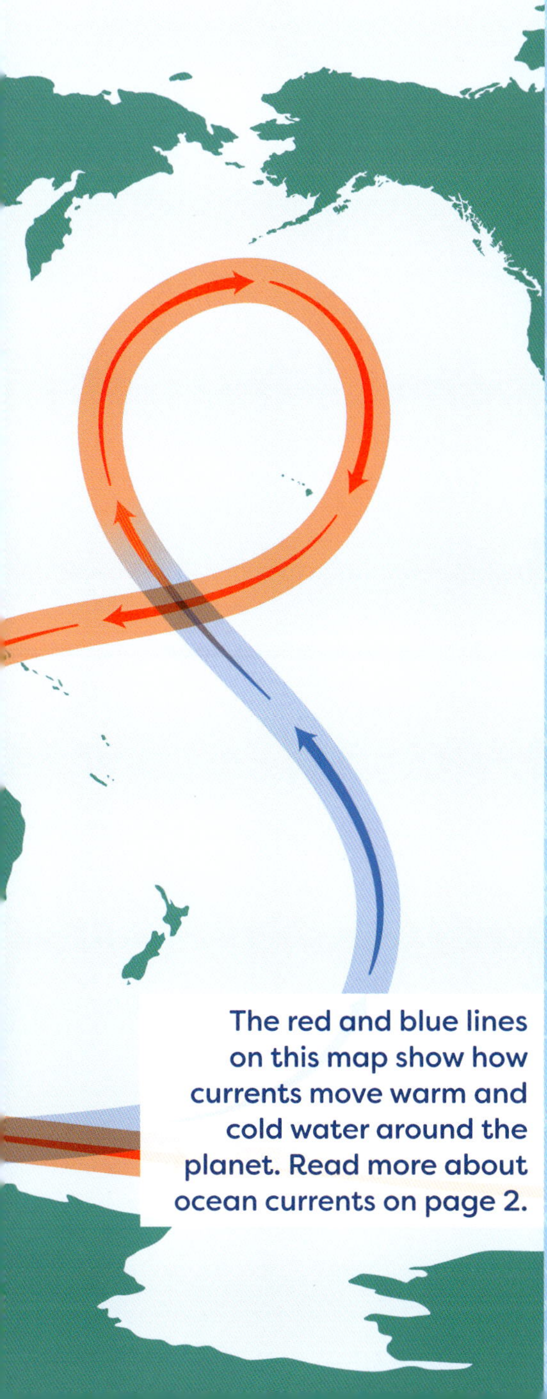

The red and blue lines on this map show how currents move warm and cold water around the planet. Read more about ocean currents on page 2.

CHAPTER ONE

THE OCEAN

Have you ever been to an ocean beach? If so, you probably felt the warm sun and the cool breeze on your skin. Maybe you smelled the salty air, dug your toes in the squishy sand, or felt the foamy waves tickle your feet. People visit the ocean to swim, surf, fish, relax, and explore, but they're just visitors. For many animals, the ocean is home.

The ocean covers about 70 percent of our planet. There are more than 320 million cubic miles of water in Earth's ocean. That's a lot of water! Scientists separate the ocean into five different areas: the Arctic Ocean, Atlantic Ocean, Indian Ocean, Pacific Ocean, and Southern Ocean. Take a look at the map of the world. Which section of the ocean is closest to where you live?

Ocean as Home

Hundreds of thousands of **species** call the ocean home. Some live buried in the sandy seafloor. Others live in coral reefs, kelp forests, or seagrass meadows. There are species that float around their whole lives and others that attach their bodies to rocks and stay put. There are even animals that live way down deep at the very bottom of the ocean.

The ocean is one giant **ecosystem**. No matter where they live in this ecosystem, marine animals depend on each other to survive. In fact, everywhere on Earth, living things are connected in big and small ways. As humans, our actions on land affect ocean **habitats** and marine life. When ecosystems are unbalanced, it can be difficult for animals to survive.

Kelp forest

Ocean Currents

The ocean is always on the move. **Currents** help animals get from place to place. They also stir up the water, which helps support ocean life and humans, too. Currents move warm water and nutrients around the planet. This constant flow of water keeps it from becoming too hot or too cold on land. In fact, without the ocean and its currents, we wouldn't be able to live on our planet at all!

Ocean Temperature

The temperature of ocean water depends on where you are. Near the equator, the surface water is warm. Near the North and South Poles, the surface water is icy and frigid. It's also very cold in the deep where sunlight can't reach. Animals can survive just about everywhere in the ocean, but as the ocean warms because of **climate change**, some animals are having trouble adjusting.

DID YOU KNOW?

Ocean life creates more than half of the oxygen we breathe on Earth.

SUPER SCIENTIST

In the 1950s, '60s, and '70s, Marie Tharp was one of the first scientists to create maps of the ocean floor. She proved it's not flat like many people thought. She used pens and rulers and information gathered by her fellow scientist Bruce Heezen to show that the bottom of the ocean has deep canyons and tall mountains.

Marie's maps showed a big crack in the seafloor surrounded by a volcanic mountain chain called the mid-ocean ridge. This crack is more than 40,000 miles long. To travel that distance, you'd have to drive across the United States about 14 times! Marie also helped scientists better understand how the seafloor moves and changes over time.

Ocean Zones

The ocean has layers, like an enormous cake. The top layer is called the sunlight zone. In this zone, the sun provides light and warmth. Most ocean animals live here. Below the sunlight zone is the darker twilight zone, followed by the even darker midnight zone. Some animals in this zone have never seen sunlight. Below it is the deep, dark abyss (abyssal zone). Finally, the trench layer (hadal zone) makes up the very bottom of the ocean cake.

Believe it or not, some types of animals, like crabs, worms, and sea stars (or starfish), live in both shallow *and* deep waters. The animals that live in the ocean's deepest places have special traits, like large eyes that can see in very low light, to help them survive.

DID YOU KNOW?
The blue whale is the biggest animal that has ever lived. It can dive as deep as 1,640 feet (500 meters) and swim as fast as 30 miles per hour.

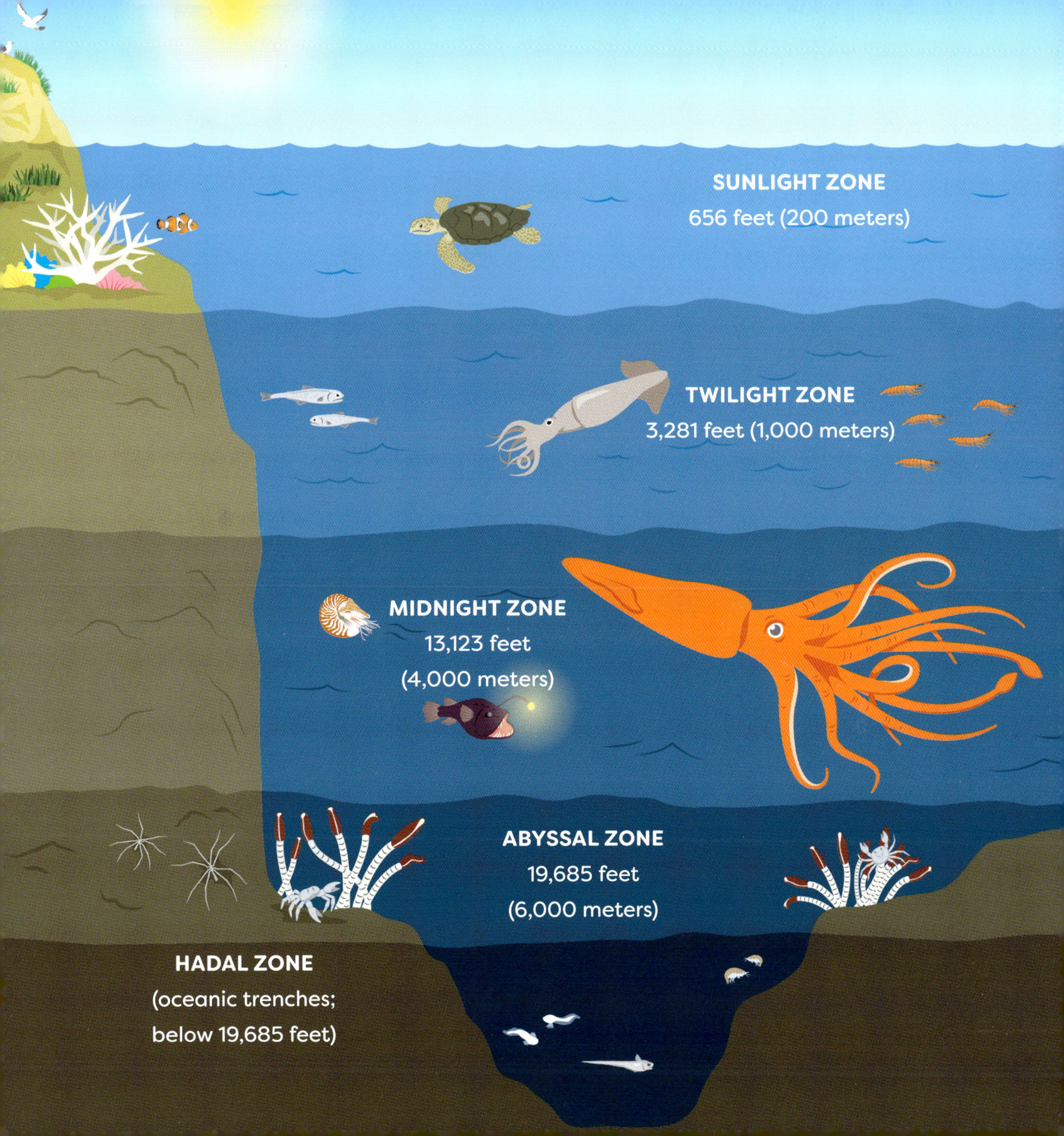
SUNLIGHT ZONE
656 feet (200 meters)
TWILIGHT ZONE
3,281 feet (1,000 meters)
MIDNIGHT ZONE
13,123 feet
(4,000 meters)
ABYSSAL ZONE
19,685 feet
(6,000 meters)
HADAL ZONE
(oceanic trenches;
below 19,685 feet)

Weddell seal, page 21

CHAPTER TWO

MARINE MAMMALS AND SEABIRDS

Like humans, marine mammals are **warm-blooded**. They breathe air, make sounds underwater, and give birth to live babies like humans do. But unlike humans, marine mammals spend most or all of their time in the ocean!

Seabirds spend a lot of time in and around the ocean, too. Some swim and others soar above the water. They eat fish and other marine animals for food and lay their eggs on land. Some seabirds fly very long distances. The wandering albatross can fly for years without touching land. Some seabirds, like penguins, don't fly at all.

Where They Live

Humpback whale surfacing to breathe through its blowholes

Marine mammals live in both warm and cold waters. Many live near the shore but visit the open ocean, too. Some, like walruses and sea lions, also spend time on land. A few marine mammals, like sperm whales, Cuvier's beaked whales, and Weddell seals, dive down deep to hunt for food.

When seabirds land, they often choose rocky shores and sea cliffs. Some seabirds, like black guillemots and Arctic skuas, prefer cold places. Others, like magnificent frigatebirds and blue-footed boobies, prefer warm places.

How They Breathe

Marine mammals and seabirds have lungs for breathing. When swimming, they must come to the surface to take a breath of air through their nostrils. Seabirds have nostrils on their beaks. Some marine mammals, like seals, sea otters, and manatees, have nostrils on their snouts. Other marine mammals, like whales, breathe through special nostrils called blowholes on top of their heads. Whales with teeth have one blowhole, and whales with **baleen** have two.

How They Reproduce

Some marine mammals, like dolphins, give birth underwater. Others, like sea lions, give birth on land. Marine mammals nurse their babies after they're born. Many seabirds build a nest for their egg or eggs, guard the nest until the eggs hatch, and then take trips to the ocean to find food and bring it back to their babies.

Black-browed albatross caring for its chick

How They Keep Warm

A thick layer of fat called blubber helps marine mammals stay warm. Some marine mammals, like seals and sea lions, have both blubber and fur to stay warm. A group of marine mammals called fur seals have blubber and *two* layers of fur!

Seabirds have feathers to help keep them warm. Many seabirds use their beaks to spread waxy oils onto their feathers. This keeps cold wind and water away from their skin. Penguins in the Antarctic need a little extra protection from the cold. Emperor penguins have two layers of feathers, plus blubber.

HEARING UNDERWATER

Whales "sing" to communicate with each other across vast distances. How well can you hear underwater? Here's a simple experiment to help you find out.

ADULT SUPERVISION REQUIRED

What You'll Need

- **LARGE BUCKET**
- **SCISSORS**
- **RECYCLED PLASTIC BOTTLE (ANY SIZE) WITHOUT THE CAP**
- **2 METAL SPOONS**

1. Fill three-quarters of the bucket with water.
2. Ask an adult to cut the bottom off the plastic bottle.
3. Place the open bottom of the plastic bottle in the water. Hold your ear next to the cap opening at the top. Ask a partner to bang two spoons together underwater. Can you hear the noise? Does it sound the same as it does above water?
4. Have your partner make a few more noises while you listen (try tapping a fingernail on the side of the bucket). Compare how the same noise sounds above and below the water.

Blue Whale

Balaenoptera musculus

SAY IT! *ba-lee-NOP-terr-a MOOS-cue-luss*

Blue whales can hear other blue whales' calls from hundreds of miles away. Because they're so big, these giants need to eat a lot of food. They mostly eat small, shrimp-like animals called krill—as much as six tons a day!

A newborn blue whale is more than 20 feet long and weighs 5,000 or more pounds. Like human babies, blue whale calves drink milk for several months after they're born. How much milk do you think a blue whale calf drinks each day? At least 50 gallons! Scientists study blue whales' earwax to estimate their age and learn more about how they live their lives.

SEA LIFE STATS

HABITAT: Open ocean

SIZE: 80 to 110 feet

WEIGHT: 200,000 to 300,000 pounds

DIET: Krill

RANGE: Everywhere except the Arctic Ocean

LIFE SPAN: Up to 90 years

Bottlenose Dolphin

Tursiops truncatus

SAY IT! *TERR-see-opps trun-CAY-tis*

Bottlenose dolphins live in groups called pods, and they work together to hunt fish and squid. They make noises that sound like clicks and whistles to talk to each other underwater. Dolphins are very playful. They like to chase each other, swim alongside boats, and leap out of the water just for fun.

Dolphins often sleep while swimming. A sleeping, swimming dolphin glides along with one eye shut and one eye open. Only half its brain sleeps at a time so the dolphin can remember to surface for air. A dolphin sheds its skin about every two hours. This keeps the dolphin nice and smooth so it can swim fast.

SEA LIFE STATS

HABITAT: Coastal areas, open ocean

SIZE: 6 to 13 feet

WEIGHT: Up to 1,400 pounds

DIET: Fish, squid

RANGE: Atlantic, Pacific, and Indian Oceans

LIFE SPAN: Up to 50 years

California Sea Lion

Zalophus californianus

SAY IT! *zah-LO-fuss CAH-lee-for-nee-ay-nuss*

Sea lions are like puppies of the sea—they have tons of energy and love to play! They use their long front flippers to get around on land and to propel themselves through the water. Sea lions are noisy. They can chuff, grunt, growl, and howl, but the most common sea lion sound is a loud bark. Mom sea lions use a special call just for their pups.

Sea lions are different from seals. Seals don't bark, and their flippers aren't as helpful for moving on land. They must scoot instead of walk. Sea lions also have flaps of skin over their ears, and seals don't.

SEA LIFE STATS

HABITAT: Coastal waters

SIZE: 6 to 8 feet

WEIGHT: Up to 800 pounds

DIET: Fish, squid, octopus

RANGE: Pacific Ocean, along the North American coast

LIFE SPAN: 20 to 30 years

Sea Otter

Enhydra lutris

SAY IT! *enn-HY-druh LOO-triss*

Sea otters have thick fur instead of blubber like most marine mammals. There arc up to one million hairs per square inch on an otter's body! Two layers of fur (an undercoat and a layer of guard hairs) help keep sea otters' skin warm and dry, even while they swim. For extra protection against the cold, they do somersaults in the water to trap air bubbles between their layers of fur. The bubbles keep the cold water off the otters' skin. To keep their fur clean, sea otters spend a lot of time grooming. They use their paws to comb their entire coat.

Sea otters snack all day long to get the energy they need to swim and keep warm. They use rocks to crack open the hard shells of clams and other **prey**.

SEA LIFE STATS

HABITAT: Kelp forests, coastal areas

SIZE: 3 to 5 feet

WEIGHT: Up to 90 pounds

DIET: Sea urchins, crabs, clams, other marine invertebrates

RANGE: Pacific Ocean

LIFE SPAN: Up to 23 years

West Indian Manatee

Trichechus manatus latirostris

SAY IT! *try-KEE-kuss MAN-ah-tuss lah-ti-ROSS-triss*

A manatee uses its strong upper lip to grab slippery seagrass and pull it into its mouth. Since a manatee doesn't have fingers, this is very helpful! Manatees live in warm, shallow places near coasts. They can also live in rivers and places called estuaries. The water in estuaries is a mix of salty ocean water and non-salty **freshwater**.

Manatees usually swim slowly. They gently paddle their rounded tail and flippers to glide peacefully through the water. In very shallow water, a manatee might use its flippers to walk along the bottom. Manatees have whiskers on their faces and hairs on their bodies. Green algae often grows on their wrinkly gray skin.

SEA LIFE STATS

HABITAT: Shallow coastal areas, rivers, estuaries

SIZE: 8 to 13 feet

WEIGHT: Up to 1,300 pounds

DIET: Seagrass

RANGE: Florida coastlines, Gulf Coast, northeast South American coast, Caribbean Sea

LIFE SPAN: About 40 years

Pacific Walrus

Odobenus rosmarus divergens

SAY IT! *oh-do-BEE-nuss rose-MARE-uss dye-VER-jens*

There's no mistaking a walrus, with its blubbery body, whiskery mustache, and long white tusks. The walrus's blubber helps it stay warm in cold water. Its mustache isn't just a fashion statement. The thick hairs help the walrus sense food like shellfish as it digs around the seafloor. And those long white tusks are really gigantic teeth!

Pacific walruses live near and on sea ice in the Arctic. They use their tusks to keep holes open in the ice so they can come up to breathe while hunting underwater. Their tusks also come in handy when they need to pull themselves out of the water and onto the slippery ice.

SEA LIFE STATS

HABITAT: Coastal areas, sea ice

SIZE: 7 to 12 feet

WEIGHT: Up to 4,000 pounds

DIET: Shellfish, other marine invertebrates

RANGE: Arctic Ocean

LIFE SPAN: Up to 40 years

Polar Bear

Ursus maritimus

SAY IT! *UR-suss mare-ih-TY-muss*

Polar bears may look white, but their hairs are actually clear and hollow. Their fur appears white because it reflects light. Underneath that fur, polar bear skin is black! Polar bears are excellent swimmers. Their webbed front paws are as big as dinner plates.

In the Arctic, polar bears are apex **predators**. This means no other animal hunts and eats them. This powerful animal eats mostly seals. When a seal pops through a hole in the ice to take a breath, a hungry polar bear may try to grab it. Hunting for seals is hard work. Most of the time, the seal escapes and the polar bear must keep trying.

SEA LIFE STATS

HABITAT: Arctic ice sheets, Arctic coastlines

SIZE: 6 to 10 feet

WEIGHT: Up to 1,400 pounds

DIET: Seals, other mammals

RANGE: Arctic Circle (Arctic Ocean and surrounding land)

LIFE SPAN: 25 to 30 years

Narwhal

Monodon monoceros

SAY IT! *MON-oh-don mon-oh-SARE-uss*

A male narwhal has one spiraled tusk sticking straight out of its face—kind of like a unicorn with its single, twisty horn. There's one big difference between unicorns and narwhals, though. Narwhals actually exist! The narwhal's tusk is really a tooth that grows through the animal's upper lip. Some male narwhals end up with two tusks, and a handful of females grow a tusk, too.

Narwhals make sound underwater to communicate with other narwhals. They also use sound to locate prey and sense their surroundings. This ability is called echolocation, and other toothed whales (including dolphins) use it as well.

SEA LIFE STATS

HABITAT: Coastal waters, often beneath Arctic sea ice

SIZE: Up to 16 feet

WEIGHT: Up to 3,200 pounds

DIET: Fish, squid, shrimp

RANGE: Arctic Ocean

LIFE SPAN: Up to 50 years

Atlantic Puffin

Fratercula arctica

SAY IT! *fah-TERR-cue-luh ARC-tik-ah*

Puffins got the nickname "clowns of the sea" because their faces look painted. But those bright colors serve a purpose—they help puffins attract other puffins! For this reason, puffins' reddish-orange feet and colorful beaks are extra bright during **breeding season**. When puffins find their mates, they bob their heads up and down and tap their beaks together. Puffins dig burrows and make nests for their eggs in cliffs or rocky areas.

When it's not breeding season, puffins spend most of their time at sea, resting and even sleeping on the surface of the water. These seabirds are great swimmers and divers. They dive, then use their wings and webbed feet to swim as they chase fish.

SEA LIFE STATS

HABITAT: Coastlines, rocky cliffs (breeding season); open ocean (nonbreeding season)

SIZE: 10 inches

WEIGHT: Just over 1 pound

DIET: Fish, marine invertebrates

RANGE: North Atlantic Ocean

LIFE SPAN: 30 to 40 years

Adélie Penguin

Pygoscelis adeliae

SAY IT! *PYE-goh-sell-iss uh-DEL-ee-ay*

Small but mighty, Adélie penguins are cute animals with an attitude. When building their nests, some Adélie penguins steal rocks from their neighbors. They may also pick fights with larger animals, like emperor penguins, and fight back against predators. The Adélie penguin's black and white feathers are a type of **camouflage** called countershading. This is when the animal's belly is light and its back is dark.

Adélie penguins live in huge groups called colonies. So many Adélie penguins live together in these colonies that astronauts can see their pink poop stains on the ground from space! Their poop is pink because Adélie penguins eat krill, which are pinkish in color.

SEA LIFE STATS

HABITAT: Rocky Antarctic coasts, pack ice

SIZE: Up to 2 feet

WEIGHT: Up to 10 pounds

DIET: Krill, fish, squid

RANGE: Antarctica, Southern Ocean

LIFE SPAN: Up to 20 years

Weddell Seal

Leptonychotes weddellii

SAY IT! *lep-tun-ee-coats weh-DELL-ee-eye*

Weddell seals can stay underwater for more than an hour while they search for food at depths of 1,000 feet (or more) beneath the Antarctic ice. To breathe, Weddell seals come back up to the water's surface and look for holes in the ice. Weddell seals use their front teeth to keep breathing holes open, which can be tricky in such cold weather, because openings often freeze over quickly.

Weddell seals haul out on the ice to rest, molt (shed their fur), and give birth. On land, they often lie on their sides. Weddell seals are named after James Weddell, a 19th-century British explorer.

SEA LIFE STATS

HABITAT: Southern Ocean

SIZE: 9 to 10 feet

WEIGHT: Up to 1,100 pounds

DIET: Fish and invertebrates like squid, octopus, and prawns

RANGE: Southern Ocean and ice surrounding Antarctica

LIFE SPAN: Up to 25 years

Whale shark, page 33

CHAPTER THREE

FISH

Fish come in all shapes and sizes—from the bus-sized whale shark to the fingernail-sized pygmy seahorse. Some are as flat as pancakes, and others can puff themselves up like balloons. There are fish with stripes, fish with spots, and fish with spikes. There are fish that "fly" across the surface of the water, fish that clean other fishes' teeth, and even fish that glow in the dark. Some, like the reef stonefish, are **venomous**. Others, like the marbled electric ray, give their prey an electric shock.

Fish are **vertebrates**. They use their senses of taste, smell, hearing, and sight to survive. Fish also have a special group of organs on their sides called the lateral line that help them sense pressure, movement, and vibrations in the water.

Where They Live

Fish live in every ocean layer, including the deepest depths. Some fish **migrate** from place to place using ocean currents. You may be able to guess where a fish lives just by looking at it. For example, a brightly colored fish may live in a place that's also brightly colored, like a tropical coral reef. A fish with very large eyes may live in a place that's dark.

Coral reef

How They Breathe

Fish have gills that allow them to breathe underwater. Gills pull oxygen out of the water, and the fish's blood delivers it to the rest of its body. A freshwater fish called the Australian lungfish has both gills and a lung, so it can breathe above and below the water!

How They Reproduce

Salmon eggs

Most fish lay a bunch of tiny eggs all at once. Only a few of those eggs survive to become adult fish. Fish that live in shallow water may lay sticky eggs among plants or rocks. Some fish even build nests for their eggs.

Sharks are fish, too. Some lay eggs, while others give birth to live babies. Great white shark moms are pregnant for 12 or more months before having a litter of up to 10 pups.

How They Keep Warm

Almost all fish are **cold-blooded** and must move to warmer water if their bodies get too cold. Scientists are learning that there may be some warm-blooded fish species, including the Atlantic bluefin tuna and a flat, round fish called the opah.

BATHTUB OCEAN

The mixing of warm and cold water creates some ocean currents. Try it out in the bathtub!

ADULT SUPERVISION REQUIRED

What You'll Need

ICE
THERMOMETER
DRIED BASIL FLAKES
MEASURING CUP
DARK FOOD COLORING
POT OR KETTLE

1. Fill a bathtub with 2 inches of cold water, and add enough ice to bring the water temperature down between 45°F and 50°F.
2. Sprinkle some dried basil flakes on the cold water to represent fish in the ocean.
3. Mix about 6 drops of dark food coloring with about 4 cups of water in a pot.
4. Ask an adult to boil the water.
5. Have an adult help you pour the hot water into the bathtub. (If the hot water isn't dark enough to see, add more food coloring.)
6. Watch how the hot water moves and mixes with the cold water. Do you see any little swirls? In the ocean, these are called eddies. As the hot and cold water mix to create currents, do the "fish" move, too?

Leafy Sea Dragon

Phycodurus eques

SAY IT! *fye-koh-DURR-uss EK-wiss*

Off the coast of Australia, leafy sea dragons hide from predators in plain sight. These unique fish look a lot like seaweed and blend right in! Since they're weak swimmers, leafy sea dragons rely on camouflage to stay safe. Sea dragons have long snouts and no teeth. They suck up their food—mostly **plankton** and tiny shrimp—like little vacuums.

Leafy sea dragons are related to seahorses. In both species, males, not females, give birth to babies. The male seahorse carries his eggs in a stomach pouch until they hatch. The male leafy sea dragon has a special spot to carry eggs on the underside of his tail.

SEA LIFE STATS

HABITAT: Rocky reefs, seagrass meadows, kelp forests

SIZE: 14 inches

WEIGHT: Less than 1 pound

DIET: Plankton, shrimp

RANGE: Southern Australian coastline

LIFE SPAN: Up to 10 years

Orange Clownfish

Amphiprion percula

SAY IT! *AM-fee-pry-on PERK-yoo-lah*

Orange clownfish are bright orange with three white stripes surrounded by black borders. Other clownfish species aren't orange at all. They can be black, brown, yellow, or maroon with white stripes. Orange clownfish live among the stinging tentacles of sea anemones. A layer of slime called mucus protects them from being stung. Predators won't risk being stung, so the anemone acts like a shield and keeps the clownfish safe.

Within a group of clownfish, the largest fish is female and the rest are male. *All* orange clownfish are male when they are born. When a group's female dies, the largest male becomes a female.

SEA LIFE STATS

HABITAT: Tropical coral reefs

SIZE: 4.5 inches

WEIGHT: 8 to 9 ounces

DIET: Algae, plankton

RANGE: Indo-Pacific region (Indian and Pacific Oceans)

LIFE SPAN: Up to 10 years

Atlantic Bluefin Tuna

Thunnus thynnus

SAY IT! *TON-nuss TIE-nuss*

Hungry, hungry tunas grow from tiny to huge during their lifetimes. Atlantic bluefin tunas can weigh up to 1,500 pounds. That's as much as a horse! They are also super speedy and can swim more than 40 miles per hour. They pull in some of their fins to become more torpedo-like as they dart through the ocean. These tunas hunt small fish like herring and mackerel and swallow them whole.

The Atlantic bluefin tuna isn't truly cold-blooded like most other fish. This species can keep its body temperature higher than its surrounding environment. This helps it move fast in cold water.

SEA LIFE STATS

HABITAT: Open ocean

SIZE: 6 to 12 feet

WEIGHT: Up to 1,500 pounds

DIET: Herring, mackerel, other fish

RANGE: Western Atlantic Ocean

LIFE SPAN: Up to 20 years

Giant Manta Ray

Manta birostris

SAY IT! *MAN-tuh bye-ROSS-triss*

Some people call manta rays "devil fish," but mantas are gentle and even friendly with human divers. So why do they have this nickname? Giant manta rays have two forward-facing fins—one on each side of their heads—that look a little like horns. A giant manta eats by swimming with its mouth open. Its gills filter the manta's favorite food—plankton—out of the water. The hornlike fins help direct food into its wide-open mouth.

Giant manta rays have giant brains. These smart fish may be able to recognize themselves in a mirror. Only a few animal species seem to be able to do this. Chimpanzees and orangutans are two of the other animals that can.

SEA LIFE STATS

HABITAT: Open ocean

SIZE: Up to 23 feet

WEIGHT: Up to 5,300 pounds

DIET: Plankton

RANGE: Atlantic and Pacific Oceans

LIFE SPAN: Up to 40 years

Green Moray Eel

Gymnothorax funebris

SAY IT! *JIM-no-THOR-ax foo-NEE-bris*

Green moray eels can swim forward and backward. This is an unusual ability for fish. These **nocturnal** eels spend their days sleeping and hiding in cracks and crevices near the seafloor. Their slimy, mucus-covered bodies can squeeze into really tight spaces.

A green moray eel's body is actually brownish or gray. It's the mucus that makes it look green! At night, this eel will sit still in the darkness, mouth open, and wait for prey to pass by. When it does, the moray snaps its jaws shut and sinks its sharp teeth into its next meal.

SEA LIFE STATS

HABITAT: Coral reefs, mangroves, rocky shorelines

SIZE: Up to 8 feet

WEIGHT: Up to 65 pounds

DIET: Fish, crabs, shrimp, squid, octopus

RANGE: Western Atlantic Ocean

LIFE SPAN: Varies, possibly 30 years or more

Tiger Shark

Galeocerdo cuvier

SAY IT! *GAL-ee-oh-sair-doh COO-vee-ay*

Tiger sharks are famous for eating just about anything they can catch. Some tiger sharks have even eaten things like car tires, license plates, and other plastic and metal garbage that gets swept out into the ocean. This can make them sick. Sharks have an amazing sense of smell. They also have an extra sense that can detect other animals in the water by picking up the electricity their bodies create as they move.

Young tiger sharks have dark stripes on their bodies that fade as they get older. These sharks have sharp teeth that are jagged like knives. Their teeth's zigzagged edges help the sharks grab and hang on to their prey.

SEA LIFE STATS

HABITAT: Coastal areas

SIZE: Up to 18 feet

WEIGHT: Up to 2,000 pounds

DIET: Almost anything—fish, other sharks, marine mammals, birds, squid, sea turtles, and more

RANGE: Worldwide in warm water

LIFE SPAN: 15 years

Whale Shark

Rhincodon typus

SAY IT! *rine-co-don TY-puss*

The whale shark isn't a whale—it's a huge shark! In fact, whale sharks are the biggest fish in the sea. Each whale shark has a unique pattern of spots, like a human's fingerprints, and scientists can use the shark's spots to identify individuals. Whale sharks typically live alone, but sometimes a huge school of them will gather to feed.

Whale sharks have huge mouths (up to 4 feet across). They open their mouths wide to gather plankton and small fish, which they filter out of the water and swallow. They have more than 300 rows of tiny, pointy teeth that they don't use.

SEA LIFE STATS

HABITAT: Open ocean

SIZE: 18 to 33 feet, or more

WEIGHT: Up to 20 tons

DIET: Plankton, small fish

RANGE: Tropical areas of the Atlantic, Indian, and Pacific Oceans

LIFE SPAN: Up to 100 years

Yellow-lipped sea krait, page 43

CHAPTER FOUR

MARINE REPTILES

Snakes, lizards, turtles, tortoises, alligators, and crocodiles are all reptiles. Most reptiles live on land and in freshwater ecosystems, but there are some—the marine reptiles—that spend part or all of their lives in the salty ocean. Marine reptiles include sea snakes and sea kraits, sea turtles, and even one species of iguana.

Sea kraits are a group of venomous sea snakes that can live in the water *and* on land. In water, a sea krait uses its paddle-like tail to swim. On the ground, sea kraits slither to move just like land-dwelling snakes. Sea kraits live in shallow water, often near coral reefs. They don't have gills, so they must come up to the surface to breathe air.

Where They Live

Many marine reptiles live near the shore in warm, shallow places like coral reefs and seagrass meadows. These are places where food is easy to find. Most sea turtles migrate from their favorite feeding spots to places where they lay their eggs. This is usually the same area where they were born!

How They Breathe

Reptiles have lungs and breathe air. Marine reptiles must hold their breath underwater and come up to the surface to breathe. Sea snakes can stay underwater for hours at a time! Blood vessels in a sea snake's head take oxygen from the water to help the animal stay underwater for so long.

DID YOU KNOW?

The largest marine reptiles known to science were ichthyosaurs (*ick-THEE-oh-sores*). These **extinct** creatures were up to 85 feet long!

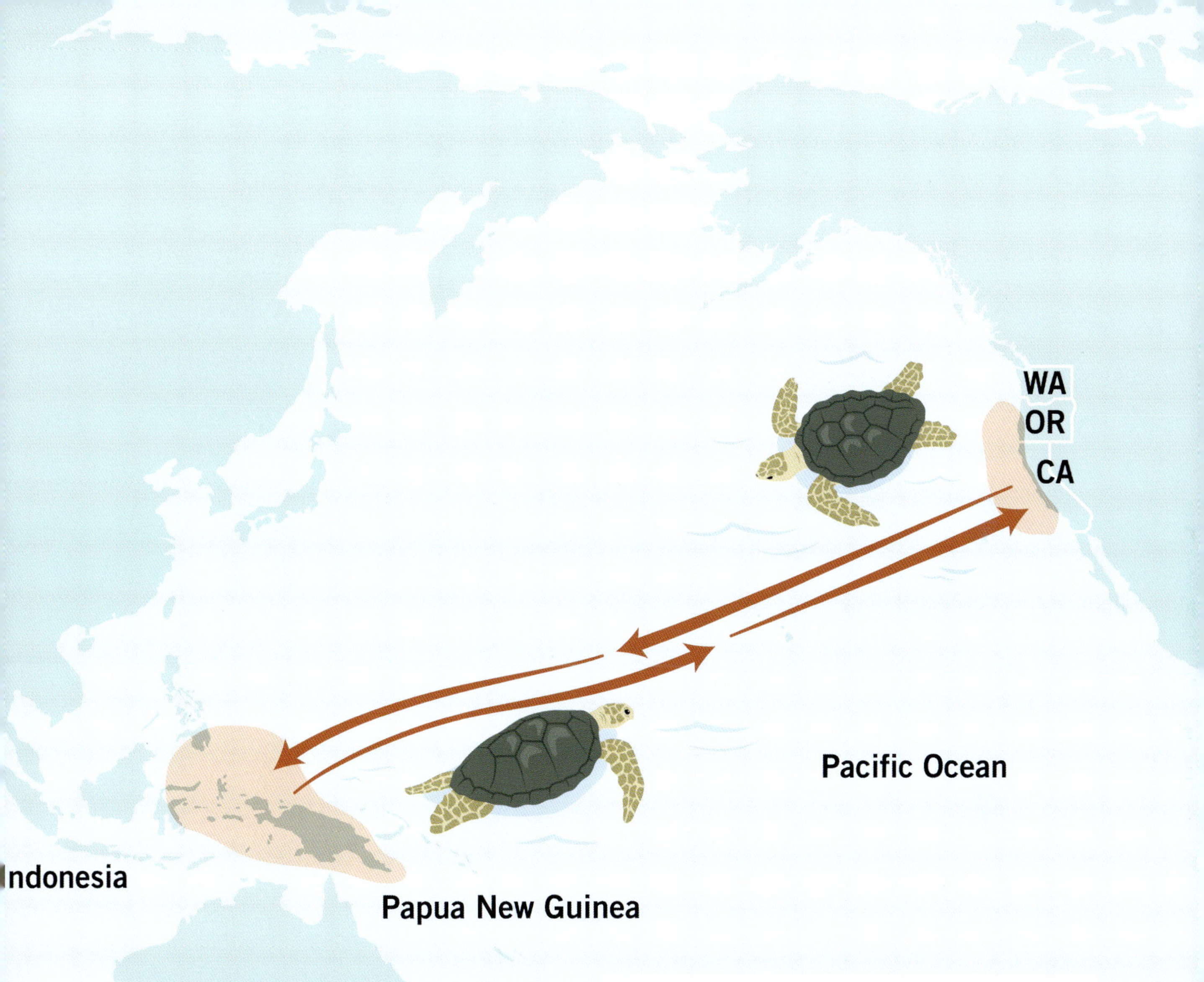

Western Pacific leatherback turtles migrate thousands of miles between California, where they feed, and Papua New Guinea, where they lay their eggs.

How They Reproduce

Many marine reptiles lay eggs. Sea kraits, sea turtles, and marine iguanas come ashore to make nests for their eggs. When the eggs hatch, the babies must get to the ocean. Sometimes it's a dangerous trek! Instead of laying eggs, most sea snakes give birth to live babies in the water.

Sea turtle eggs

How They Keep Warm

Almost all reptiles are cold-blooded. To keep warm, marine reptiles tend to stay in warmer waters. Since marine iguanas can come ashore, they often lie on rocks and bask in the sun to warm up after diving in the ocean.

Yellow-Bellied Sea Snake

Hydrophis platurus

SAY IT! *HYE-droh-fiss plah-TURR-uss*

Most sea snakes live in shallow water, but the yellow-bellied sea snake spends its time swimming in the open ocean or drifting on ocean currents. It floats on the surface, waiting for fish to swim underneath and then it strikes. Yellow-bellied sea snakes have short fangs that inject venom into their prey. Their bright yellow bellies and patterned tails warn other animals to stay away.

Just like snakes on land, sea snakes have scales and shed their skin. The yellow-bellied sea snake twists itself into a knot and wiggles around to rub off its old skin. Sea snakes can't drink salty seawater, so where do they find freshwater in the middle of the ocean? They drink the rainwater that floats on the surface of the ocean after a big storm.

SEA LIFE STATS

HABITAT: Open ocean

SIZE: 2 to 3 feet long

WEIGHT: Less than 1 pound

DIET: Fish

RANGE: Pacific and Indian Oceans

LIFE SPAN: Up to 3 years

Hawksbill Sea Turtle

Eretmochelys imbricata

SAY IT! *err-ETT-moh-keel-iss IMM-bri-kata*

Sea turtles have long front flippers and webbed feet for swimming. Hawksbill sea turtles have oval shells made of tough, bony scales called scutes. The hawksbill's pointed beak helps it reach into small spaces to grab its favorite food—sea sponges.

Hawksbills are good at finding their way through the ocean. A sea turtle's brain acts like a compass and points the turtle in the right direction. When ready, a female hawksbill travels back to the beach where she was born, digs her body into the sand, and lays up to 160 eggs at a time. If the nest is warm, most hatchlings will be female. If it's cool, most hatchlings will be male.

SEA LIFE STATS

HABITAT: Coral reefs, seagrass meadows, mangroves, other shallow habitats

SIZE: 2 to 3 feet long

WEIGHT: Up to 150 pounds

DIET: Sea sponges, sea anemones, sea jellies (jellyfish), algae

RANGE: Atlantic, Indian, and Pacific Oceans

LIFE SPAN: Unknown, but possibly up to 50 years

Leatherback Turtle

Dermochelys coriacea

SAY IT! *durr-mo-KEEL-iss kor-ee-UH-see-uh*

Can you imagine a turtle that weighs more than a cow? Leatherbacks can weigh 2,000 pounds! The leatherback gets its name from its unique rubbery shell, which doesn't have bony scutes like other sea turtles' shells. Leatherbacks travel farther and dive deeper than other sea turtles. They can also handle cooler water temperatures because they have a layer of fat to help keep them warm.

Leatherbacks like to eat sea jellies. Sometimes they eat plastic bags floating in the ocean because they look like jellies. This makes the turtles sick. Many sea turtles are **endangered**, because they mistake trash for food, get caught in fishing nets, or get hit by boats. Some humans also take turtle eggs from nests to eat or sell.

SEA LIFE STATS

HABITAT: Open ocean

SIZE: 4.5 to 5.5 feet long

WEIGHT: Up to 2,000 pounds

DIET: Sea jellies

RANGE: Atlantic, Indian, and Pacific Oceans

LIFE SPAN: Unknown, but possibly up to 45 years

Marine Iguana

Amblyrhynchus cristatus

SAY IT! *am-blee-RINK-uss kriss-TAY-tuss*

There's only one species of lizard swimming around the ocean: the marine iguana. Marine iguanas love to eat algae and dive down to scrape this yummy treat from rocks. Sharp claws help them grasp the rocks and crawl along the seafloor. Their flat tails act like paddles to help them swim. Many marine iguanas are dark colored or almost black, but some are reddish, greenish, or turquoise. Males are more colorful than females.

Because marine iguanas eat algae, there is a lot of salt in their diet. Special glands near a marine iguana's nose clean the extra salt from its blood so the iguana can "sneeze" it out! After a "sneeze," salt goes flying and lands on the iguana's face and head. When the salt dries, it looks white and crusty.

SEA LIFE STATS

HABITAT: Rocky shorelines

SIZE: Up to 5 feet long

WEIGHT: Up to 3 pounds

DIET: Algae

RANGE: Galápagos Islands (Pacific Ocean)

LIFE SPAN: Up to 12 years

Yellow-Lipped Sea Krait

Laticauda colubrina

SAY IT! *LAT-ih-ka-da CAW-luh-BREE-na*

Also known as the banded sea krait because of its dark bands or stripes, the yellow-lipped sea krait gets its name for its yellow snout. Sea kraits use venom to paralyze their prey before they swallow it whole. Then they go ashore to digest, which can take several weeks. Yellow-lipped sea kraits prefer to eat eels. Interestingly, females are larger than males and tend to eat much larger prey, like conger eels.

On land, the yellow-lipped sea krait may spend time in low tree branches. In the ocean, they can stay underwater for almost two hours while they hunt.

SEA LIFE STATS

HABITAT: Coral reefs and rocky shorelines

SIZE: Up to 4 feet long

WEIGHT: Unknown

DIET: Eels, small fish

RANGE: Indo-Pacific region (Indian and Pacific Oceans)

LIFE SPAN: Unknown

Cuttlefish

CHAPTER FIVE

MARINE INVERTEBRATES

There are millions of animals in the ocean that don't have backbones. These cool creatures are called **invertebrates**. Invertebrates in the ocean include crabs, lobsters, oysters, squids, sea stars, sea cucumbers, sea anemones, and corals.

How do marine invertebrates protect themselves? Some, like marine snails, have hard casings called **exoskeletons** to protect their soft bodies from predators. Others, like cuttlefish, hide by changing color to match their environment. Box jellies and blue-ringed octopuses are both dangerously venomous. Sea cucumbers have one of the weirdest defenses on the planet. They can eject organs out of their backsides!

Where They Live

You can see invertebrates like sea anemones, sea stars, and sea urchins at the beach if you live near a place with tide pools—puddles left behind when the tide goes out. Marine invertebrates live everywhere in the ocean, from tide pools on rocky beaches down to the deepest ocean trenches. In the deep sea, you'll find invertebrates like sea jellies that glow in the dark, worms that live in tubes, and even giant squid.

Giant green anemones in a tide pool

How They Breathe

Some marine invertebrates have gills to breathe underwater. Others don't. Sea sponges and many other marine invertebrates have small openings called pores that take oxygen from the water. Sea spiders "breathe" through pores in their legs! Sea stars and related animals take oxygen into their bodies through their suction-cup feet.

How They Reproduce

Some marine invertebrates reproduce by cloning themselves or by dividing their bodies in half. Sea anemones, sea jellies, and corals can all do this! Many other marine invertebrates lay eggs. A female octopus protects her eggs until they hatch. She won't even leave the eggs to hunt!

What They Eat

Giant clam on the ocean floor

Marine invertebrates eat everything from plankton to other invertebrates and even large fish. Some bottom-dwelling shrimp and crabs feast on the bodies of animals that have died and sunk to the seafloor. Others don't really need to eat at all. Giant clams are the world's heaviest invertebrates, and they get much of their energy from the algae living inside their bodies. The algae turn sunlight into energy and pass some of this energy on to the clam. In return, the clam provides a good, safe home for the algae.

A DEEPER LOOK

What are tides? As the Moon circles Earth and Earth circles the Sun, the Sun and Moon both pull on our planet (thanks to gravity) and create ocean tides. The Moon is mostly responsible for Earth's tides because it's much closer to the Earth than the Sun is, and therefore it has a stronger gravitational pull.

During high tide, the water comes farther up on the beach, possibly forcing you to move all your beach gear so it doesn't get wet. At low tide, the water gets pulled back and exposes more of the beach. Exploring the beach during low tide is a great way to see marine invertebrates, especially if there are tide pools!

Tide pool

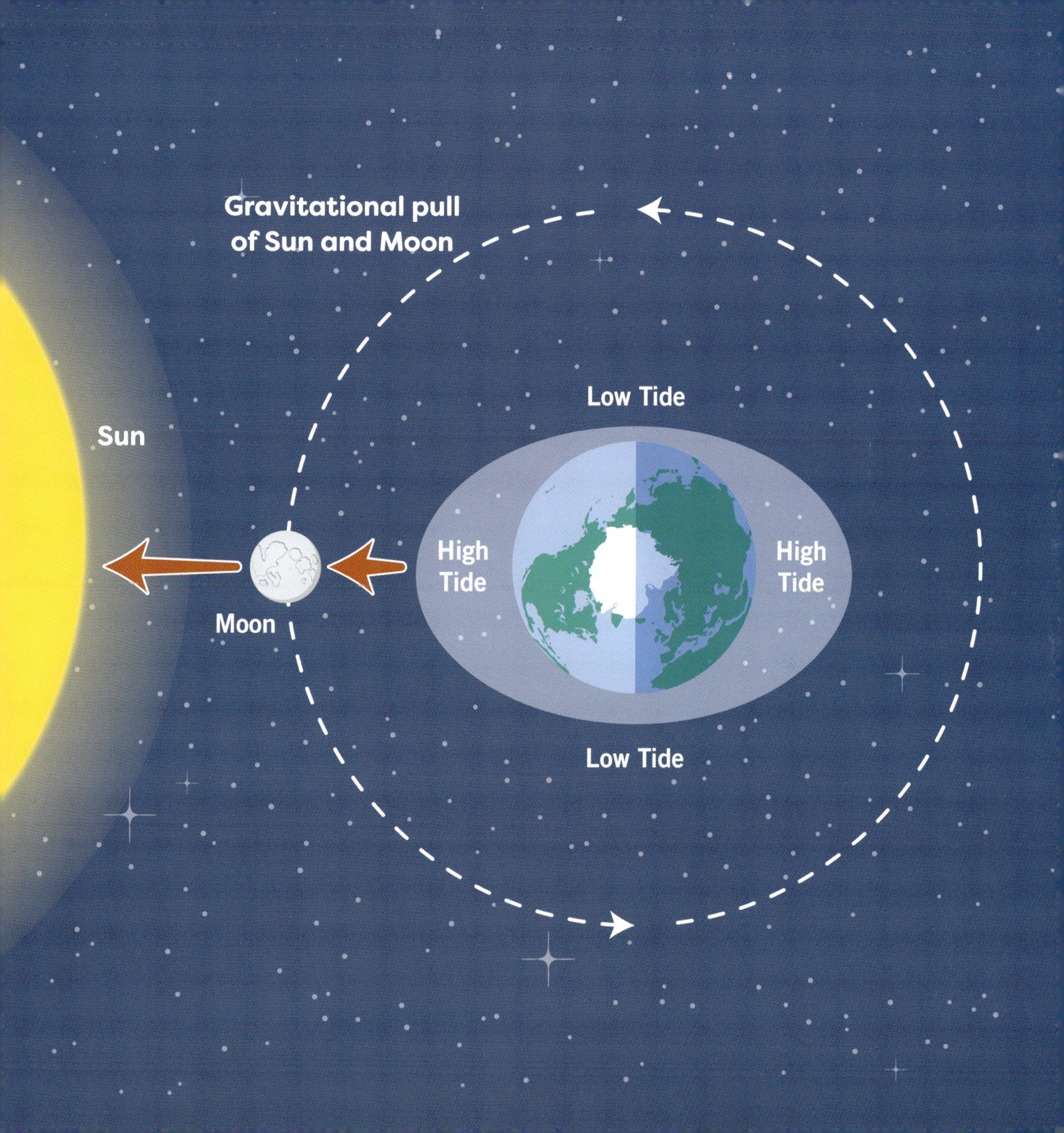
Gravitational pull
of Sun and Moon
Sun
Moon
Low Tide
High
Tide
High
Tide
Low Tide

Giant Sea Spider

Colossendeis megalonyx

SAY IT! *call-us-sen-DAY-iss MEG-uh-lonn-iks*

Compared to most sea spiders, the giant sea spider is huge. It can be nearly 2 feet long! Scientists think they grow bigger than other sea spiders because they live in very cold, very deep places. Giant sea spiders have eight long legs that they use to swim or walk along the seafloor. There is not much else to their bodies. Even their organs are in their legs! Male sea spiders carry eggs on their legs until they hatch.

Sea spiders are related to land spiders, but they aren't true spiders. Giant sea spiders feed on other animals, like pom-pom anemones, by sucking out their prey's body fluids through their straw-like mouths.

SEA LIFE STATS

HABITAT: Deep sea

SIZE: Up to 20 inches long

WEIGHT: Unknown

DIET: Anemones, other invertebrates

RANGE: Southern Ocean

LIFE SPAN: Unknown

Lion's Mane Jellyfish

Cyanea capillata

SAY IT! *SY-uh-nay-uh CAP-ih-lah-tah*

Jellyfish should really be called sea jellies, since they're invertebrates, not fish. Sea jellies are mostly made of water. They don't have blood, hearts, or brains. They move by pulsing instead of swimming and often travel along with ocean currents.

The lion's mane jelly's body has an umbrella-like bell (or body) and tentacles that can be 120 feet long! It uses its tentacles full of stinging cells to capture prey like small fish and other sea jellies. If you watch these stinging cells fire under a microscope, it looks like tiny needles shooting out and injecting venom into the sea jelly's victim.

SEA LIFE STATS

HABITAT: Open ocean

SIZE: Up to 8 feet wide (bell) and 120 feet long (tentacles)

WEIGHT: More than 400 pounds

DIET: Plankton, small fish, small invertebrates, other sea jellies

RANGE: North Pacific, North Atlantic, and Arctic Oceans

LIFE SPAN: Less than a year

Staghorn Coral

Acropora cervicornis

SAY IT! *uh-CROP-or-uh sur-vih-COR-niss*

Staghorn corals are alive, even though they look more like sculptures than animals. The structures you see when you look at a coral reef are the stony skeletons of tiny animals called polyps. Coral polyps have soft bodies. They rely on their hard exoskeletons for protection. The polyps build their exoskeletons on top of other polyps' exoskeletons. Over time, they create coral reefs where lots of fish and other marine life like to live. A group of staghorn corals is called a thicket.

Staghorn coral polyps have algae living inside their bodies that help keep them healthy. Rising ocean temperatures can cause the algae to leave their coral hosts. This weakens the corals and turns them white. Scientists call this process coral bleaching.

SEA LIFE STATS

HABITAT: Warm, shallow water

SIZE: 8 or more feet long and 4 or more feet high

WEIGHT: Varies

DIET: Plankton

RANGE: Caribbean Sea

LIFE SPAN: Hundreds of years

Blue Sea Star

Linckia laevigata

SAY IT! *LINK-ee-uh lay-vuh-GAH-tah*

Blue sea stars have five arms with rounded tips and hundreds of tube feet on their undersides. These tube feet suction to rocks and other surfaces to keep the sea star from being swept away by waves. Some sea star species have more than 20 arms!

The sea star's arms and tube feet help it sense the world around it. On the tip of each arm is an eyespot, which helps the sea star sense light. Blue sea stars can regrow an arm if it is snatched by a predator. To eat, the sea star bends over its food, drops its stomach out of its mouth, and starts digesting the food outside of its body.

SEA LIFE STATS

HABITAT: Shallow water habitats like coral reefs and tide pools

SIZE: Up to 16 inches

WEIGHT: Less than 1 pound

DIET: Algae, other marine invertebrates, dead animals

RANGE: Indo-Pacific region (Indian and Pacific Oceans)

LIFE SPAN: 10 years

Orange Fan Sponge

Stylissa flabelliformis

SAY IT! *sty-LISS-ah fluh-BELL-ih-form-iss*

It doesn't move, but an orange fan sponge is still an interesting marine invertebrate. Yup—marine sponges are animals, not plants! Baby orange fan sponges, called larvae, drift around until they find the perfect place to live. Once they do, they attach themselves to the rocky seafloor and stay there for the rest of their lives.

Sponges don't need to move, because the ocean does all the work for them. Water full of food (plankton), oxygen, and other goodies constantly flows through pores in the sponges' bodies. The sponges filter what they need to survive right out of the water. This is called filter feeding.

SEA LIFE STATS

HABITAT: Coastal rocky areas, coral reefs

SIZE: Varies

WEIGHT: Varies

DIET: Plankton

RANGE: Indo-Pacific region (Indian and Pacific Oceans)

LIFE SPAN: Unknown

Giant Hermit Crab

Petrochirus diogenes

SAY IT! *pet-ro-KY-russ dye-AH-jen-eez*

A hermit crab without a shell is like a fish out of water—exposed and unprotected. Hermit crabs borrow (and sometimes steal) other animals' shells to protect their soft bodies. As the crabs grow, they must move into bigger and bigger shells. A giant hermit crab will eat the animal inside a shell if it wants to use the shell as a home! Groups of hermit crabs also gather together to exchange shells, but sometimes they fight over the best ones.

Giant hermit crabs are red and large compared to other hermit crabs. They have one big claw and one small claw. Hermit crabs use their big claws in many ways, including for self-defense.

SEA LIFE STATS

HABITAT: Muddy or sandy seafloors, seagrass, coral reefs

SIZE: Up to 11 inches

WEIGHT: Possibly up to 10 pounds

DIET: Other invertebrates, algae

RANGE: Caribbean Sea, Gulf of Mexico, surrounding areas in the Atlantic Ocean

LIFE SPAN: Varies, possibly up to 40 years

Chambered Nautilus

Nautilus pompilius

SAY IT! *NOT-ih-luss pom-PILL-ee-uss*

Can you guess what this animal is? Is it a huge snail? A strange sort of squid? It's called a chambered nautilus, and it's related to octopuses and squids. A chambered nautilus can swim forward and backward by shooting water through a tube near its head. This type of movement is called jet propulsion. It can pull its body, including its 90 or so tentacles, completely into its shell for protection.

Nautiluses often hang out in deep waters near coral reefs during the day and come up to shallower waters at night to hunt. These animals can't see very well, so they use their sense of smell to find and capture prey.

SEA LIFE STATS

HABITAT: Coral reefs

SIZE: Up to 9 inches

WEIGHT: 2 or more pounds

DIET: Fish, other invertebrates like crabs and shrimp, dead animals

RANGE: Western Pacific Ocean

LIFE SPAN: Up to 20 years

Peacock Mantis Shrimp

Odontodactylus scyllarus

SAY IT! *oh-DON-to-dak-till-uss sci-LARE-uss*

Meet the peacock mantis shrimp, a colorful but deadly marine predator. It may be small, but this shrimp has a pair of secret weapons—two clubs built to smash. Most of the time, a peacock mantis shrimp's clubs are neatly tucked away on the sides of its body. When they are needed, this powerful puncher extends its clubs at an amazing 50 miles per hour, striking its target with incredible force. The shrimp hits hard enough to break through the shells of its prey.

The peacock mantis shrimp can rotate its eyes separately and look in two directions at once! These shrimp can see more types of light than humans can. Their advanced eyes are perfectly suited for underwater life.

SEA LIFE STATS

HABITAT: Shallow water, coral reefs, sandy seafloors

SIZE: Up to 7 inches

WEIGHT: About 1 pound

DIET: Snails, other marine invertebrates

RANGE: Indo-Pacific region (Indian and Pacific Oceans)

LIFE SPAN: Up to 6 years

Giant Pacific Octopus

Enteroctopus dofleini

SAY IT! *en-terr-OCK-toe-pus DOH-flee-nigh*

Three hearts, eight arms, thousands of superstrong suckers, and blue blood. This may sound like a creature from another planet, but it's not—it's a giant Pacific octopus! Most of an octopus's body is soft, but it has a hard beak that it uses to bite and tear its prey. Because it is mostly squishy, a giant Pacific octopus can squeeze into tiny places. A female giant Pacific octopus lays many thousands of eggs inside her underwater cave or den and then protects them until they hatch. She will even blow bubbles over the eggs to keep them clean.

Giant Pacific octopuses can solve basic puzzles, open jars, and even recognize different people. In fact, they may be the smartest invertebrates on Earth.

SEA LIFE STATS

HABITAT: Coastal areas

SIZE: Up to 16 feet

WEIGHT: Up to 150 pounds

DIET: Shrimp, crabs, clams, other marine invertebrates, fish

RANGE: Northern Pacific Ocean

LIFE SPAN: 3 to 5 years

Humboldt Squid

Dosidicus gigas

SAY IT! *dose-ID-ikus GUY-gass*

Humboldt squid grow to be the size of an adult man and can weigh more than 100 pounds. (Interestingly, the plural of *squid* when talking about more than one individual of a single species is *squid*, not *squids*!) These large squid are **bioluminescent**. They put on light shows in the deep sea, often flashing their whole body red and white to communicate with each other. Like other squid species, Humboldt squid have eight arms full of suckers and two tentacles. Their tentacles have suckers lined with sharp teeth that help them snatch prey.

Humboldt squid hunt in groups. They take turns swimming in a spiral path upward through schools of fish. When threatened by predators, they release a cloud of dark ink to distract their foes and make a daring escape.

SEA LIFE STATS

HABITAT: Open ocean, deep sea

SIZE: Up to 6 feet

WEIGHT: Up to 110 pounds

DIET: Small fish, small squid, crustaceans

RANGE: Eastern Pacific Ocean

LIFE SPAN: 1 to 2 years

Blue whales, page 11

MORE TO DISCOVER

WEBSITES

The Marine Mammal Center
MarineMammalCenter.org
A great site for learning more about marine mammals

MarineBio Kids
MarineBio.org/marinebio/games
Collection of online resources, games, and puzzles for kids interested in marine biology

National Geographic Kids
kids.NationalGeographic.com
Fun animal facts, videos, and games

National Oceanic and Atmospheric Association (NOAA) for Kids
OceanService.NOAA.gov/kids
Resources and activities for kids and students of all ages

BOOKS

Marine Science for Kids: Exploring and Protecting Our Watery World, by Bethanie and Josh Hestermann

This book gives advanced readers an in-depth look at the world of marine science and includes 21 hands-on activities.

National Geographic Kids Ultimate Oceanpedia: The Most Complete Ocean Reference Ever, by Christina Wilsdon

This ocean reference book for kids is filled with fabulous photos, diagrams, and fun facts.

Shark Lady: The True Story of How Eugenie Clark Became the Ocean's Most Fearless Scientist, by Jess Keating

This book tells the true story of how one young girl fell in love with sharks and grew up to become known as the "Shark Lady."

ORGANIZATIONS

Association of Zoos and Aquariums (AZA)

AZA.org

A nonprofit organization that promotes conservation, education, science, and recreation

Monterey Bay Aquarium Research Institute (MBARI)

MBARI.org

An institute that conducts ocean research using the latest technology

Polar Bears International

PolarBearsInternational.org

An organization dedicated to wild polar bears and Arctic wildlife conservation

Woods Hole Oceanographic Institution (WHOI)

WHOI.edu

Advances knowledge of the ocean and its connection to our planet

GLOSSARY

BALEEN: Stiff plates inside some whales' mouths that filter plankton from ocean water

BIOLUMINESCENT: Possessing the ability to create light

BREEDING SEASON: The time of year when males and females of a species come together to mate and produce babies

CAMOUFLAGE: The ability to hide by blending in with or matching the background

CLIMATE CHANGE: A gradual change in Earth's average conditions, such as rainfall and temperature

COLD-BLOODED: Having a body temperature that matches the temperature of the surrounding air or water

CURRENT: The movement of water from one place to another in the ocean caused by wind, tides, or other forces

ECOSYSTEM: A community of different living things that interact with each other and their surroundings

ENDANGERED: At risk of going extinct and disappearing from the wild

EXOSKELETON: A hard casing on the outside of an animal's body

EXTINCT: No longer living on Earth

FRESHWATER: Non-salty water, such as the water in rivers and lakes

HABITAT: The place in which an animal lives

INVERTEBRATE: Having no backbone

MARINE: Having to do with the ocean

MIGRATE: To travel from one place to another at the same times each year

NOCTURNAL: Active at night

PLANKTON: Small plants and animals that drift or float in the ocean

PREDATOR: An animal that eats other animals for food

PREY: An animal that other animals eat for food

SPECIES: A group of living things that have a lot in common and can make others of their kind

VENOMOUS: Containing a harmful substance called venom that is used to injure other animals, usually by bite or sting

VERTEBRATE: Having a backbone

WARM-BLOODED: Having the same body temperature all the time, even if the surrounding air or water temperature changes

INDEX

ACKNOWLEDGMENTS

Special thanks to Emily Yam, Talia Dietrich, and Chris Mah for help with scientific name pronunciations.

ABOUT THE AUTHORS

Bethanie and **Josh Hestermann** are authors of animal-science books for kids. They've written *Zoology for Kids: Understanding and Working with Animals*, *Marine Science for Kids: Exploring and Protecting Our Watery World*, *Search the Ocean: Find the Animals*, and *Search the Zoo: Find the Animals*. Bethanie is a freelance writer, and Josh is a zoologist working at the Orange County Zoo. They have two children.